THE SKILLS, MENTALITY, & FAITH
NEEDED TO BE GREAT IN SALES

RELENTLESS SALES

RESOURCE GUIDE

JON ALWINSON

FORGE PRESS

This publication is designed to provide accurate and authoritative information in regard to the subject matter covered. It is sold with the understanding that the publisher is not engaged in rendering legal, accounting, or other professional service. If legal advice or other expert assistance is required, the services of a competent professional person should be sought.

Library Of Congress Cataloging-In-Publication Data

Alwinson, Jon. Relentless sales: official resource guide / by Jon Alwinson

ISBN 979-8-9892254-1-5. 1. Sales.

2. Faith. 3. Mentality. I. Title.

Edited by Zach Swee

Book Design by Keane Fine

TABLE OF CONTENTS

CHAPTER 1: MENTORS

KEY CONCEPTS:

1. The Impact of Mentoring:

   - Mentoring can make a significant difference in one's personal and professional life.

   - Focusing on strengths had a transformative effect on the Jon Alwinson's career trajectory.

2. The Role of Mentors in Career Development:

   - Mentors play a crucial role in career development by providing guidance, support, and a network of connections.

   - Networking with successful individuals can open up opportunities and contribute to personal and professional growth.

3. The "Board of Directors" Concept:

   - Create a "Board of Directors" for one's life, consisting of respected individuals with high character and achievements.

   - These mentors can provide valuable advice on various aspects of life, contributing to a solid foundation for personal and professional growth.

4. Long-Term Mindset:

   - Encouragement to think with a long-term mindset, live with character, and focus on meaningful relationships with mentors.

   - Acknowledgment of the importance of these qualities in building a career on a solid foundation.

ACTION STEPS:

1. Identifying Potential Mentors:

   - Reflect on your network and identify individuals who could serve as mentors.

   - Make a shortlist and say a prayer over your choices:

     _____

     _____

     _____

     _____

2. Board of Directors:

   - List below prospective names of your personal "Board of Directors:"

     _____

     _____

     _____

     _____

REFLECTION:

- Reflect on your true desire to succeed in sales and life and let it fuel your commitment to building a mentorship network.

DISCUSSION QUESTIONS

1. What are your strengths and how can you leverage them in your career or personal life?

2. Jon felt pressure to stabilize his career and make important decisions. Have you ever felt pressure to conform to certain expectations or timelines in your professional or personal life? How did you balance it?

3. Share your thoughts on the importance of mentors. Have you actively sought out mentors in your life or career? If yes, what benefits have you experienced?

4. What do you think about the concept of creating a "Board of Directors" for your life, consisting of mentors and advisors? Can you identify individuals in your network who could serve on such a board?

CHAPTER 2: IDENTITY

KEY CONCEPTS:

1. Foundation of Success:

   - One's identity is the foundation of success.

   - Timothy Keller: "Identity grounded in Christ rather than work."

2. Living from Identity, Not for Identity:

   - "Live *from* your identity, not *for* your identity."

     ◦ Shift in perspective from work-centric success to understanding a broader identity.

3. Balancing Priorities:

   - Acknowledgment of the need to balance professional goals with personal identity, relationships with God, and family.

   - Living as a son of God first, irrespective of professional success.

4. Freedom in Identity:

   - Understanding the concept of being "enough" as one is, irrespective of professional achievements.

   - The liberating effect of aligning one's identity with a higher purpose.

     ◦ "My opinion of me should be growing out of God's opinion of me."

5. Competitive Advantage in Sales:

   - Linking a Christ-centered identity to a competitive advantage in sales.

   - Building a confident, humble, and likable spirit that fosters authentic relationships with customers.

6. Openly Sharing Faith:

   - Encouragement to openly talk about God and share the hope and power found in faith.

- Challenging the societal conditioning that discourages discussing faith in business settings.

ACTION STEPS:

1. Daily Reminder:

   - Write the phrase "Live from your identity" on a 3 x 5 card and carry it with you all week.

   - Read the phrase multiple times per day as a reminder of the importance of identity.

REFLECTION:

- Reflect on a time when you felt most "free" and connected to God.

- Before important sales calls, think about your identity, smile, and enter the meeting with the confidence of being a loved son or daughter of God.

DISCUSSION QUESTIONS:

1. How would you describe your own sense of identity, especially in relation to your work or career? Do you find that your identity is closely tied to your professional success?

2. Jon mentions a perspective shift in his life when he was advised to "live from your identity, not for your identity." Have you ever experienced a similar shift in perspective that significantly impacted your approach to work or life?

3. Discuss the challenge of balancing professional ambitions with personal identity. How can one pursue career success without letting it define their sense of self-worth?

4. The chapter emphasizes aligning one's identity with God. How does faith or spirituality play a role in shaping your identity, and how might it influence your approach to work?

5. How do you think personal values and identity can impact your professional relationships and success?

CHAPTER 3: GO ALL-OUT

KEY CONCEPTS:

1. Importance of Massive Action:

    - Tony Robbins: "The path to success is to take massive, determined action."

    - Life is short, and individuals are advised to go all-out to make the most of their opportunities.

2. Short Window for Impact:

    - Emphasis on the short window of opportunity to make an impact within an organization.

    - Advice to start fast and give an all-out effort early in a sales career or when joining a new organization.

3. Risk and Reward:

    - Recognition that success involves risks and sometimes moving away from one's comfort zone.

    - Recognition that success may open doors to unexpected opportunities.

4. Unpredictable Career Changes:

    - Sales and business environment are unpredictable.

    - The need to stay ready, trust in God, and consistently put in excellent work.

5. Relentless Mentality:

    - The belief that consistent effort, grit, and a never-give-up mentality create a competitive advantage.

ACTION STEPS:

1. Career Evaluation:

    - Use the provided "Weekend Planner" from www.JonAlwinson.com to plan and evaluate your career.

    - Consider whether it's time to go all-out or make adjustments in your career.

REFLECTION:

1. Everybody's Sore, Tired, and Has Excuses:

   - Reflect on the quote by Lewis Caralla: "Everybody's Sore. Everybody's Tired. Everybody has an excuse. Don't be Everybody."

   - Consider how embracing a relentless mentality can set you apart in the competitive field of sales.

DISCUSSION QUESTIONS:

1. Share a personal or professional challenge you faced that required you to give your best effort. How did you approach it, and what was the outcome?

2. Jon discusses taking a significant risk by leaving a Fortune 500 company for a startup. How do you evaluate and balance risks and opportunities in your career?

3. How have moments of adversity shaped your professional journey and how did you overcome challenges?

4. Discuss the idea that being ready for opportunities requires continuous effort. How do you stay prepared for unexpected opportunities in your career?

5. How do you maintain motivation and a strong work ethic throughout the ups and downs of your career?

CHAPTER 4: CONFIDENCE

KEY CONCEPTS

1. Source of Confidence:

   - Robert Kiyosaki: "Confidence is linked to discipline and training"

   - The pivotal role of confidence in sales is highlighted: customers want to buy from people they like and trust.

   - The advice to be authentic and build trust by instilling confidence in customers.

   - Focus on strengths rather than solely attempting to improve weaknesses.

2. Confidence Pendulum:

   - Common extremes in the confidence spectrum for salespeople: overconfidence (arrogance) or lack of confidence (self-doubt).

3. Self-Awareness and Coaching:

   - Importance of self-awareness in sales.

   - Coaching to individual strengths, with an example comparing Achievers and those wired for competition.

4. Humility as a Confidence Builder:

   - Defining humility and recognizing its importance in building confidence.

   - Humility as a foundational virtue and a solid foundation for life and business.

5. Productive Working Habits:

   - The role of daily effort, highly productive working habits, and a positive mindset in building and growing confidence.

   - The need to believe in oneself and maintain a strong belief system for success.

6. Avoiding Negative Habits:

   - The observation of negative habits in sales counterparts, such as slowing down and complaining.

ACTION STEPS:

Self-Assessment:

- Take a personality test, spiritual gifts test, or strengths-based test.

- Review the results with someone respected to gain additional perspectives.

REFLECTION:

- Reflect on the wisdom from Proverbs 14:26: "In the fear of the Lord one has strong confidence."

- Consider how faith and humility contribute to genuine confidence in sales.

DISCUSSION QUESTIONS:

1. How does the book define confidence in the context of sales? Why is confidence considered a crucial factor for success in sales?

2. The chapter mentions the common extremes of overconfidence and lack of confidence in salespeople. Have you observed colleagues on either end of this spectrum? How did it affect their performance?

3. How does self-awareness of strengths and weaknesses contribute to building confidence? Share examples from your own experiences.

4. Discuss the role of highly productive working habits in building and growing confidence. How do daily efforts and disciplined habits contribute to success in sales?

5. How can you balance confidence and humility in your approach to sales? Share strategies for maintaining a confident yet humble demeanor.

CHAPTER 5: RELATIONSHIPS > EVERYTHING

KEY CONCEPTS:

1. Customer-Centric Mindset:

   - The importance of putting the customer's needs first and never manipulate.

   - The responsibility of salespeople is to be difference-makers, creating a positive environment.

   - Position customers as heroes in their stories.

     ○ Guide helping customers navigate challenges.

2. Connecting on a Personal Level:

   - The best salespeople connect with customers at a relational level before delving into business.

   - Emphasis on listening, understanding needs, and offering solutions that genuinely benefit customers.

   - The power of a smile and intentional relationship-building habits.

3. Planning and Intentionality:

   - The need for strategic thinking, planning, and gathering facts before meeting with customers.

   - The importance of slowing down, especially for high-energy individuals.

4. Motives and Positive Intentions:

   - The recognition that customers can discern genuine motives.

   - The significance of being customer-focused, humble, and open-minded in discussions.

   - The impact of expressing genuine praise and appreciation to customers.

ACTION STEPS:

1. Continuous Improvement:

   • Set reminders to prioritize customers, fostering the habit of putting them first.

REFLECTION:

1. Customer-Centric Success:

   • Consider Ray Kroc's quote: "If you work just for money, you'll never make it, but if you love what you're doing and you always put the customer first, success will be yours."

   • Reflect on how a customer-centric approach can lead to sustained success.

DISCUSSION QUESTIONS:

1. Discuss the role of relationships in sales. How does the chapter define successful relationship-building, and why is it considered crucial for sales professionals?

2. Think about a major purchase you made. How did the sales professional approach your needs? Discuss the impact of a salesperson focusing on your needs versus pushing their own agenda.

3. Explore the concept of making customers the heroes of their journey. How does this perspective shift benefit both the salesperson and the customer?

4. How can acknowledging and praising individuals within an organization contribute to building strong relationships?

5. How can sales professionals ensure that their customer-first mindset is genuine and not manipulative?

CHAPTER 6: DEVELOP AN ELITE SALES PROCESS

KEY CONCEPTS:

1. Art and Science of Sales:

    - Sales involves both art (soft skills, intuition) and science (skill set, knowledge).

    - Developing an elite sales process requires a balance of these elements.

2. Adaptability in Sales Process:

    - Great salespeople adapt their process to serve customer needs.

    - An elite sales process provides clarity throughout the sales journey.

3. Importance of Sales Process:

    - An effective sales process guides and directs salespeople throughout engagements.

    - Consistency in sales is achieved through a well-structured and repeatable sales process.

    - A good sales process helps understand the customer's buying cycle.

    - Continuous improvement is crucial for sharpening sales skills.

The MATRIX (MX®) Sales Process: Pre-Call Planning, Approach, Identify Pain, Demonstrate Value, Advance, Close, Follow-Up:

- Pre-Call Planning:

    - Research prospective customers before engagement.

        ○ Utilize websites, social media, CRM, and organization data.

- Approaching with Rapport:

    - Genuine smile, genuine interest, warm engagement, and relationship-building.

- Identifying Pain:

    - Pain is the reason customers buy; salespeople are problem solvers.

- Demonstrating Value:

    - Slow down, ask questions, and understand the extent of customer pain.

    - Demonstrate value in alignment with the customer's needs.

- Advancing the Sale:

    - Confidently guide customers to the next steps in the sales process.

    - Tailor the approach based on individual customer needs and preferences.

- Closing - Asking for the Business:

    - Demonstrate real value before asking for the business.

    - Recap the value offering, express confidence, and outline next steps.

ACTION STEPS:

- Define Your Sales Process:

    - Practice defining your sales process in a simple, bullet-point format:

    _____

    _____

    _____

    _____

    _____

    _____

    _____

    _____

REFLECTION:

- Consistency in Sales Production:

    - Reflect on the analogy of shooting form in basketball and its correlation with consistency in sales production.

DISCUSSION QUESTIONS:

1. Discuss the significance of having an elite sales process. How does a structured approach contribute to consistency and success in sales?

2. How do great salespeople adapt their sales process to serve the needs of customers? Share examples of this being done well.

3. Share experiences where understanding the customer's buying cycle was crucial in sales. How does a good sales process help in assessing where the customer is in the buying journey?

4. Discuss the importance of pre-call planning in the sales process. How can thorough research and preparation impact the success of a sales interaction? Share tips for effective pre-call planning.

5. Why is understanding the customer's pain crucial, and how does it drive the sales conversation? Share experiences related to pain identification.

CHAPTER 7: ORGANIZE FIRST, THEN TAKE MASSIVE ACTION!

KEY CONCEPTS:

1. Importance of Systems:

   - James Clear: "You do not rise to the level of your goals. You fall to the level of your systems."

   - Emphasizes the significance of having effective systems in place.

2. The Zoned Territory Sheet:

   - Creating an organized document for all accounts in the sales territory.

   - Different from CRM, it focuses on winning new revenue and staying hyper-focused.

3. Focus on Existing Customers:

   - Prioritize existing customers as the best customers.

   - Implement the 80/20 Rule (Pareto Principle) to maximize effectiveness.

4. Weekly Attack List:

   - Develop a list of opportunities with a high probability of closing.

   - Systematically work through the list, prioritizing based on closing probability.

5. Weekly Planning Session:

   - Allocate dedicated time weekly for planning.

   - Saturday planning sessions can provide a relaxed environment for effective planning.

6. Sales Tools and Vehicle Organization:

   - Sales tools, samples, and the vehicle are crucial for outside B2B sales.

   - Emphasizes the importance of maintaining a clean and organized vehicle.

7. Discipline and Excellence:

- Commit to excellence in organization as a key skill for sales success.

- Set reminders and utilize email features to stay organized.

ACTION STEPS:

- Create Zoned Territory Sheet and Weekly Attack List:

  - Work on creating these tools today to experience the positive impact on your business.

REFLECTION:

- Reflect on Lincoln's quote: "If I only had an hour to chop down a tree, I would spend the first 45 minutes sharpening my axe."

- What is your level of organization and areas where you may be able to provide focus to improve?

DISCUSSION QUESTIONS:

1. How did the realization about the lack of organization impact Jon early in his sales career? Can you relate to a similar experience in your professional life?

2. Reflect on the idea of creating a Weekly Attack List. How does this approach help in prioritizing tasks and opportunities?

3. Discuss the relevance of the 80/20 Rule in sales, especially in identifying and focusing on top customers. How can this principle guide sales professionals in allocating their time and efforts effectively?

4. Why does Jon emphasize the importance of keeping sales documents, samples, and the vehicle consistently organized? How does the organization contribute to a salesperson's success?

5. Share your thoughts on dedicating at least one hour per week to planning. How do you ensure that you maintain discipline in organizing and planning amid a busy schedule?

CHAPTER 8: OWNING THE MENTAL GAME

KEY CONCEPTS:

1. Control over Attitude and Effort:

   - Emphasis on personal responsibility for attitude and effort.

2. Mental Toughness:

   - Importance of mental toughness for sustained success.

   - Salespeople often face self-sabotage due to lacking mental resilience.

3. Documenting Wins:

   - Document personal wins to build mental fortitude.

   - Adopt the concept of a mental "cookie jar" for storing past accomplishments.

   - Use past victories as motivation during challenging times.

4. Effective Daily Disciplines:

   - Develop daily habits for mental growth and toughness.

     ○ Example: Early morning routine, goal reviews, affirmations.

5. Physical Training:

   - Physical effort contributes to mental toughness.

   - Athletes' discipline in training parallels success in sales.

6. Building a Proper Mental Framework:

   - Care less about others' opinions; focus on self-improvement.

   - Rooting identity in God for freedom from fear of others' judgment.

   - Develop self-awareness and processes to overcome the fear of criticism.

ACTION STEPS:

- Document Personal Wins:

  - Allocate time to write down personal wins and accomplishments:

    _____

    _____

    _____

    _____

- Develop Daily Disciplines:

  - Create effective daily disciplines (physical, spiritual, mental) for personal growth:

    _____

    _____

    _____

    _____

REFLECTION:

- Reflect on the foundations of your identity. What grounds you from getting too high or too low on yourself?

DISCUSSION QUESTIONS

1. How does reflecting on past successes contribute to building mental fortitude? Share examples of personal wins that have positively impacted your mindset.

2. How does Jon's morning routine contribute to mental resilience? Share your own daily disciplines that help you stay focused and mentally strong.

3. How does physical discipline contribute to persistence in challenging situations?

4. How does having a strong foundational identity contribute to overcoming the fear of judgment? Share strategies for building a mindset that cares more about personal growth than external opinions.

5. How can sales professionals distinguish between constructive feedback and baseless criticism? Share strategies for maintaining confidence and focus in the face of negativity.

6. How does faith contribute to a salesperson's ability to overcome challenges and setbacks? Share personal stories or reflections on the role of faith in your professional journey.

CHAPTER 9: CONQUERING FEAR

KEY CONCEPTS:

1. Power of Action:

   - "Inaction breeds doubt and fear. Action breeds confidence and courage."

   - Encouragement to overcome fear through proactive measures.

2. Faith as the Antidote:

   - Faith is presented as the most potent antidote to conquer fear.

   - Utilizing scripture memorization as a tool to conquer fear.

   - Recommending repeating empowering verses, e.g., Romans 8:31.

   - Positive affirmations impact mindset and communication.

3. Fear in Sales:

   - Fear in the context of sales is often linked to the opinions of others.

   - Salespeople's tendency to dwell on mistakes and fear.

   - Urgency in taking massive action to break through fear and setbacks.

   - Addressing fear by pursuing goals obsessively and persistently.

4. Self-Reflection on Authenticity:

   - Questions for self-reflection: Am I authentic, or do I seek approval?

   - Balancing authenticity and fear of judgment in business interactions.

ACTION STEPS:

- Affirmation or Scripture Practice:

  - Write down an affirmation or scripture; carry it throughout the week.

  - Read it aloud to strengthen faith muscles.

REFLECTION

- What's stopping you and holding you back from breaking through the stronghold of fear?

- What limiting beliefs are holding you back?

DISCUSSION QUESTIONS

1. How has fear impacted your professional or personal lives?

2. How is faith considered the antidote to fear? Reflect on instances where faith has helped you overcome fear or uncertainty.

3. Explore the idea that trusting in others' opinions can be a deadly trap. Share instances where external opinions influenced your actions in business or life. Discuss strategies for maintaining authenticity in the face of external judgments.

4. Share personal affirmations or phrases that have helped you overcome fear or self-doubt. Discuss the psychological and emotional impact of positive self-talk and affirmations. How can repeating affirmations contribute to building confidence?

5. Share instances where taking immediate action helped you overcome fear or challenges in your career. Discuss the balance between thoughtful planning and decisive action.

CHAPTER 10: THE SKILLS OF GREAT SALESPEOPLE

KEY CONCEPTS:

1. Relentless Prospecting:

   - Superstars are relentless, unstoppable prospectors.

   - The importance of maintaining a pipeline full of qualified prospects.

2. Skills Beyond Building Relationships:

   - Great salespeople possess skills in asking good questions and listening deeply.

   - Understanding the health of their business, spending time wisely, and remaining persistent and optimistic.

3. Customer-Centric Approach:

   - Emphasizing the need to understand and align with customers' goals.

   - Consequences of not listening and learning from customers.

   - Highlighting the value of asking clarifying questions.

4. Effective Body Language:

   - The role of positive and open body language in sales meetings.

   - The importance of avoiding negative body language and projecting a positive demeanor.

5. Meeting Framework:

   - A suggested formula for structuring meetings, including introduction, gaining understanding, digging deeper, and engagement.

   - Encouraging the development of a personalized meeting framework.

6. Deep Understanding of Business:

   - Successful salespeople possess a deep understanding of their business.

- Analytical skills to spend time wisely and maximize efforts in serving customers and markets.

- The power of using technology to analyze product mix, spending, and year-over-year growth.

- Incorporating data analysis into the Zone Territory Sheet and Weekly Attack List.

ACTION STEPS:

- Self-Assessment:

  - Identify the area among asking good questions/listening deeply, understanding your business, and remaining persistent/optimistic that requires the most improvement:

  _____

  _____

  _____

  _____

REFLECTION:

- Reflect on Thomas Edison's quote, "Our greatest weakness lies in giving up." How does this quote relate to the persistence required in sales?

DISCUSSION QUESTIONS:

1. Why is it important to understand customer goals? How can sales professionals benefit from putting themselves in their customers' shoes?

2. Discuss the negative consequences of starting a business relationship on the wrong foot. Share experiences where engaging with the wrong customers proved to be draining and time-consuming.

3. How does asking questions prevent assumptions, and why is it essential in sales? Share personal experiences where asking questions led to valuable insights and solutions.

4. Discuss the significance of positive and open body language in sales meetings. How can body language affect customer perceptions? Share tips for maintaining positive body language and avoiding negative cues during sales interactions.

5. Discuss how analytical skills contribute to effective time management and maximizing efforts. Share experiences where a profound understanding of sales numbers positively impacted decision-making.

6. Which of the three areas—asking good questions/listening deeply, deepening your understanding of your business, or remaining persistent and optimistic—do you feel you need to work on the most?

CHAPTER 11: DAILY HABITS TO WIN!

KEY CONCEPTS:

1. Compound Interest of Habits:

    - James Clear: "Habits are the compound interest of self-improvement."

    - The significance of daily habits and routines in self-improvement.

2. Owning Your Morning:

    - The importance of mastering morning routines for personal growth and improved performance.

    - Creating repeatable, positive processes to thrive through challenges.

    - Recommendations for starting the morning with a focus on a deeper energy source (Daily Appointment with God - DAWG).

        ○ Connecting to God for long-term success and personal development.

        ○ Introduction to the DAWG Guide for remembering Identity, Purpose, Character, and Confidence.

        ○ Reading a Proverbs daily for wisdom in skillful living.

3. Affirmations for Strength:

    - Building mental, emotional, and spiritual strength through meaningful affirmations.

    - The impact of positive affirmations on overcoming negativity and influencing others positively.

4. Winning Habits:

    - Developing winning habits with organizational tools and detailed planning.

    - Focusing on the top three most important tasks each day.

ACTION STEPS:

- Self-Assessment:

  - Identify the area among waking up earlier, creating an affirmation list, or spending time praying that needs the most improvement:

    _____

    _____

    _____

    _____

- Reflection

  - Reflect on Ivan Turgenev's quote, "If we wait for the moment when everything is ready, we shall never begin." How does this quote relate to the concept of taking action and implementing positive habits in daily life and sales?

DISCUSSION QUESTIONS:

1. How can a positive morning routine contribute to improved performance in a sales role?

2. Discuss the concept of the Daily Appointment with God (DAWG). How does connecting with a deeper source, such as spirituality, positively influence one's life and professional journey?

3. How do negative thoughts hinder personal and professional progress? Share strategies for overcoming negative thought patterns and fostering a positive mindset.

4. How can an organized schedule contribute to increased productivity and focus? Share tools or planners you use for staying organized and managing your daily tasks.

CHAPTER 12: ELIMINATING ENTITLEMENT

KEY CONCEPTS:

1. Entitlement Thinking:

    - Introduction to the phrase "Nobody owes you anything."

    - The importance of avoiding entitlement in sales to remain effective.

    - Creating a winning mindset through a daily reminder.

    - Anthony Iannarino: The enemy as comfort in personal and professional growth.

    - The danger of complacency and decline once reaching a comfortable level.

2. Humility and Hunger:

    - The winning formula of humility combined with a genuine desire to help customers.

    - The slippery slope to mediocrity and weakness when feeling owed by others.

ACTION STEPS:

- Self-Evaluation:

    - Rate yourself on a scale of one to ten regarding entitlement.

    - Identify one action to move one notch up on the scale.

Rating: _____

ACTION:

_____

_____

_____

_____

REFLECTION:

- Reflect on Guy Kawasaki's quote about wanting his kids to inherit a world based on merit and hard work, not entitlement. How can individuals contribute to creating such a world?

DISCUSSION QUESTIONS:

1. How did entitlement manifest in your personal or professional lives, and what impact did it have? Discuss any challenges or successes in overcoming entitlement in your personal or professional life.

2. Examine the mentality captured in Gary Vee's poster, "No One Owes You Anything." How can this mindset be beneficial for salespeople? Discuss the importance of maintaining a humble and grateful attitude.

3. How does comfort hinder personal and professional growth? Explore the idea of maintaining a growth mindset and the role of continuous improvement.

CHAPTER 13: RESPONSIBILITIES OF A SALES REP

KEY CONCEPTS:

1. Sales Fundamentals:

   - Mike Weinberg: "The core responsibilities of salespeople: CREATE, ADVANCE, and CLOSE revenue."

2. Team Collaboration:

   - The importance of building a positive work culture within a sales team.

   - Selfishness hinders success.

   - The Rule of Three: Be grateful, be positive, and share ideas with your team.

3. Sharing Insights:

   - The value of sharing feedback from the field.

   - The importance of evaluating what is working and not working collectively.

   - Being a good teammate by actively participating in a healthy team culture.

4. Continuous Learning:

   - The mindset of always being a student of the game in sales.

   - The role of reading, listening to audio recordings, and studying successful salespeople.

   - Committing to a life-long journey of learning and growth.

5. Going the Extra Mile:

   - Dabo Swinney - Doing common things in an uncommon way.

   - Standing out by being undeniably good at what you do.

   - Developing a winning mindset and being great where you are planted.

ACTION STEP:

- Team Elevation:

    - Intentionally try to elevate your sales team this week.

    - Send a Monday morning text message of encouragement, highlight a peer and the solid work they do, and/or praise instead of criticize.

    - Observe the positive changes in the team environment.

REFLECTION:

- Reflect on the mentality of "Out Plan, Out Execute, and Out Hustle your competition every day." How does this competitive mindset contribute to success in sales?

DISCUSSION QUESTIONS:

1. How does focusing on teamwork and contributing to a good work culture enhance personal and professional growth? Share experiences of positive team dynamics and discuss strategies for fostering collaboration within a sales team.

2. Reflect the Rule of Three—be grateful, be positive, and share ideas with your team. How can these principles contribute to building a positive work culture?

3. How does being self-centered limit professional and personal growth?

4. How can openness and transparency contribute to collective improvement? Share personal experiences where sharing feedback positively impacted team performance.

5. Discuss the concept of being a "student of the game" in sales. How does continuous learning contribute to excellence in sales?

6. What are strategies for staying updated on sales trends, techniques, and best practices?

7. How can small gestures, such as Monday morning text messages or praising peers, positively impact the team environment? Share ideas for fostering encouragement and collaboration within the team.

CHAPTER 14: THE POWER OF GOALS

KEY CONCEPTS:

1. The Significance of Goals:

    - Definition: "A goal is a dream with a deadline."

    - Fuel in the furnace of achievement.

    - Consequences for not having clear goals.

    - The impact of competitive nature on achieving greatness.

2. Goal Setting and Habits:

    - The habit of consistently writing and reviewing goals.

    - The importance of good habits and their compounding effect.

    - S.M.A.R.T. Goals: Specific, Measurable, Attainable, Realistic, and Time-Bound goals.

ACTION STEP:

- Goal Writing and Review:

    - Write your goals weekly and review them every day.

    - Subconsciously think about your goals and find ways to achieve them.

    - Create a balance by setting goals outside of work (Spiritual, Personal, Financial, Family, Fitness).

    - Use tools like sticky notes, and consider recording yourself stating your goals for a powerful reinforcement:

    _____

    _____

    _____

    _____

REFLECTION:

- Reflect on the concept of "Competitive Greatness" described by John Wooden. How does the competitive nature drive individuals to excel, even when faced with seemingly unbeatable competition?

DISCUSSION QUESTIONS:

1. How does the act of setting specific and measurable goals contribute to a salesperson's motivation and success? Share examples of goal-setting experiences in your professional or personal life.

2. How does confidence build over time, and what role does consistent performance and positive habits play in boosting confidence? Share personal insights on the relationship between confidence and success.

3. How do small, consistent actions over time lead to significant results? Share personal experiences where the compound effect of habits became evident.

4. How does balancing spiritual, personal, financial, family, and fitness goals contribute to overall well-being? Share examples of how a balanced goal-setting approach has positively impacted your life.

CHAPTER 15: SHOVEL THE ROCKS

KEY CONCEPTS:

1. Persistence and Mental Toughness:

    - The importance of staying the course and never giving up.

    - Reinforcement of the significance of remembering one's goals and staying positive.

    - Developing mental toughness through enduring challenges.

2. Physical Exercise for Mental Strength:

    - Correlation between physical and mental strength in sales.

    - Start a new workout program for both physical and mental fitness.

    - Jocko Willink - get up, reload, re-engage, attack

3. Sunday Night Planning:

    - The discipline of Sunday night planning

ACTION STEP:

- Physical and Mental Training:

    - Start a consistent diet and physical training program today.

    - Watch Jocko's YouTube video, "GOOD," for inspiration.

- Mental Toughness Evaluation:

    - On a scale of one to ten, evaluate your mental toughness.

    - Aim to move one level up over the next 90 days.

Rating: _____

ACTION:

_____

_____

_____

_____

REFLECTION:

- Reflect on the metaphor of shoveling rocks as a representation of the challenges in sales. How does this analogy resonate with your experiences in sales or other aspects of life?

DISCUSSION QUESTIONS:

1. Discuss the parallels between the physical challenge of shoveling rocks and the mental and emotional challenges in sales. How do the physical and mental aspects of overcoming obstacles contribute to success in sales?

2. How do endurance and persistence play a crucial role in the field of sales?

3. Consider the suggestion that physical training is beneficial for the sales game. How does physical fitness contribute to mental strength and resilience in sales?

4. Reflect on the statement that sales, while not war, is often a tough environment. How do you navigate the challenges and toughness of the sales landscape? Share strategies for remaining authentic, caring about customers, and developing mental fortitude in sales.

5. Discuss the importance of balancing work and personal life, with a focus on being obsessive about staying ahead in sales. How do you find a balance between work and personal life while striving for excellence in your professional career?

6. Discuss the notion that opportunities are often created and found through challenges. How do you approach challenging times in your professional life?

7. Share personal stories of overcoming challenges in your sales or professional journey. How did you approach difficult situations, and what lessons did you learn from overcoming obstacles? Encourage participants to share insights and strategies for overcoming challenges.

CHAPTER 16: PREPARE NOW

KEY CONCEPTS:

1. Elite Preparation in Sales:

   • Importance of creating a Career Playbook for personal and professional development.

   • Willingness to invest time in learning and documenting successful strategies and techniques.

2. Steps to Create a Personal Playbook:

   • Understanding career goals and seeking mentorship.

   • Becoming a student of the craft and studying success in the field.

   • Taking massive action and developing habits for success.

3. Three Critical Pillars for Success:

   • Fueling up early in the morning with the right mindset.

   • Being willing to put in the work during the day.

   • Putting in after-hours effort for continuous improvement.

4. Three-step Success Process:

   1. Understand where you want to go.

   2. Identify how to get there.

   3. Take massive action.

ACTION STEP:

- Create Your Personal Playbook:

    - Start today by understanding your career goals.

    - Identify how you will achieve those goals and document strategies.

    - Take massive action towards success.

Goal	Action

REFLECTION:

- Reflect on your preparation. What are ways that you can do to improve your performance through incrementally improving how you prepare?

DISCUSSION QUESTIONS:

1. What does elite preparation mean in the context of sales, and how can sales professionals adopt this mindset? Share personal experiences where meticulous preparation led to positive outcomes in sales.

2. How can sales professionals overcome laziness and fear to commit to elite preparation? Share motivational insights and personal strategies.

3. What does "massive action" entail in the context of sales, and how can individuals implement this mindset in their daily routines?

4. How does this mindset empower sales professionals to make intentional choices in their daily routines? Share examples of situations where choosing success over comfort led to positive outcomes.

CHAPTER 17: REDEFINING FAILURE

KEY CONCEPTS:

1. Embracing Failure:

    *   Recognizing failure as an essential element of striving for greatness.

    *   Balancing the need to avoid recklessness with the importance of taking bold actions.

    *   Embracing adversity and making failure a regular part of one's life.

2. Building Confidence with a Full Pipeline:

    *   The role of a full pipeline in reducing fears and building confidence.

    *   The power of action in overcoming sales challenges.

3. Learning from Mistakes:

    *   Implementing a system to process and learn from failures.

    *   The value of real-time coaching in minimizing failures.

4. The Coachable Mindset:

    *   The importance of being coachable and going the extra mile.

    *   The transformative effect of being willing to take risks and face potential failures.

ACTION STEP:

*   Create a Learning Journal:

    *   Develop a "Things I Am Learning" note in your phone.

    *   Regularly record mistakes, lessons learned, and insights to track personal growth.

REFLECTION:

*   Reflect on your relationship with failure. Do you let failure become an obstacle or do you use it to fuel success? What are ways that you can make failure a stepping stone to your growth?

DISCUSSION QUESTIONS:

1. Share a personal experience from your childhood or professional life where you initially viewed failure negatively. How has your perception of failure evolved over time, and what benefits have you discovered in embracing failure?

2. How can sales professionals balance the risk of failure with the confidence that comes from putting in the work and delivering value to customers?

3. Discuss the connection between having a full pipeline of opportunities and building confidence in sales. How does a solid pipeline reduce the fear of failure, and in what ways does it contribute to an attractive confidence that is not perceived as desperation?

4. Share instances from your career where being coachable and going the extra mile made a significant impact. How can a willingness to be coached and taking additional steps contribute to both personal and professional growth?

5. How has failure contributed to your self-discovery and learning about what works and what doesn't in your professional journey?

6. How can changing our perspective on failure set us up for a lifetime of success, and what practical steps can individuals take to redefine their approach to failure?

CHAPTER 18: BE YOU

KEY CONCEPTS:

1. Overcoming Pressure to Conform:

    - The tendency to be overly concerned about what others think, especially in sales.

    - Balancing the need for positive relationships with authenticity.

2. Embracing Authenticity in Sales:

    - Encouraging authenticity in sales interactions.

    - The importance of embracing individuality and uniqueness.

3. Continual Learning and Growth:

    - Acknowledging the ongoing nature of the journey to success in sales.

    - The significance of continuous learning, mentorship, and personal development.

ACTION STEP:

- Connect and Engage:

    1. Visit http://www.jonalwinson.com/ for free resources and bonus content

    2. Jon@AlwinsonBooks.com

    3. Text: 404-272-5236 to join the weekly text thread

REFLECTION:

- Reflect on the Teddy Roosevelt quote, "People don't care how much you know until they know how much you care." How does this resonate with your approach to sales?

DISCUSSION QUESTIONS:

1. What are your thoughts on the idea that we often care too much about what others think of us, especially in the context of sales?

2. How do you perceive the balance between being authentic and trying to meet others' expectations, especially in a sales role?

3. How does the pressure of constantly trying to be "on" impact your overall well-being and performance as a salesperson?

www.ingramcontent.com/pod-product-compliance
Lightning Source LLC
Chambersburg PA
CBHW081232020426
42331CB00012B/3146